I0212456

MY GOTHIC ROMANCE

poems by

Mehnaz Sahibzada

Finishing Line Press
Georgetown, Kentucky

MY GOTHIC ROMANCE

Copyright © 2019 by Mehnaz Sahibzada
ISBN 978-1-63534-863-7 First Edition
All rights reserved under International and Pan-American Copyright Conventions.
No part of this book may be reproduced in any manner whatsoever without written
permission from the publisher, except in the case of brief quotations embodied in
critical articles and reviews.

Publisher: Leah Maines
Editor: Christen Kincaid
Cover Art and Design: Joe Moralez, image from Shutterstock
Author Photo: Mehnaz Sahibzada

Printed in the USA on acid-free paper.
Order online: www.finishinglinepress.com
            also available on amazon.com

Author inquiries and mail orders:
Finishing Line Press
P. O. Box 1626
Georgetown, Kentucky 40324
U. S. A.

Table of Contents

I: DARK

II. LIGHT

Acknowledgments

Bio

"Dark as it was getting, I could still see these changes; though as mere alterations of light and shade: for color had faded with the daylight."

—Charlotte Bronte, *Jane Eyre*

I.

DARK

ON WRITING

There are dungeons
in my mind
where the captured
sleep.

RED MOON

On my evening walk, I am the girl
with two heads—a schizoid startled
by strangers. My heart leaps like a fish.

A boatman once told me, hate swims
down the spine and becomes a wish.
Women who elope to storm center,

grow beards and make mistakes.
I stroke my chin reflexively. The moon
drips swirls of consolations. Still my

mind is a monster of menstruations.
There is a cosmos inside of me that wants
to erupt. I picture my spleen expanding,

my kidneys shooting stars. In the lawn
outside my neighbor's house, a rage of roses.
Their thorns like the fangs of a wolf.

SERPENTINE

There are runes falling out of
the sky of my palms like candy, a pinnata
split open by a blindfolded fiend with seeds
        sprouting in his throat. I wash the
dishes and picture
        his face exploding his voice stuck
in my mouth, an uncouth joke. I think
of the taste of mint the way it settles on the
        tongue cool & piercing like an argument.
I've nicknamed him
        dictator. The fabric of my dress clings
to my skin as if needing me to move
the way my mind clings to his insults
        as if each blood stained word were
true, as if women
        with soft bones were rivers to avoid like
plagues or accidents or pews or hurricanes
or homes abraded by ghosts or the pull of
        serpentine thoughts that shake loose
the wrists, pilfering runes.

THORNFIELD

Some days I wonder
if this blue mind
could be nearsighted—
there are thoughts that make
the island beyond the lake
visible—the island
where my husband lost
his sight, where the girl
I hate was bewitched
by the daughter of
a French whore.
        There are days
that make me
wonder why
I keep pacing
this castle with
my blouse unbuttoned,
skin glittering
as though madness
makes a
woman shine
her wrists two pulsing
nutmegs.
        There are vices in
me stranger than the
things this castle
has seen. Centuries
ago, I vowed
to be good. But that
was before a swamp
surfaced
in my head. Before
my mind, this pink
fruit, scraped itself
into blue.

THE WOLF

I didn't know he would follow
me home, his gaze a gloss
in the bedroom's darkness,
two full moons in a desert
sky. The world all blackness,
a reminder we subsist in a space
that's haunted. His yellow eyes
watch me sleep, as if the day we
shared evening in the garden were
the start of some knotted myth
women untangle on verandas
painted with jasmine. I have been
the wolf too, stalked home my
prey in the alchemy of my blood-
lust, invented whole histories
piled with snow. I tell the eyes,
you watch me watching. The
whole planet's an encounter
between virgin and vice. But
though my words are wind, he does
not blink. Each night my bedroom
quakes like a wilderness of trees.

BLACK WIDOW

I keep the bedroom door
locked. The lamp
on my nightstand barely
glows. All evening long,
the rain pours haikus.
The hallway seems
a throughway for ghosts.

A book of spells
lies open on my
bedspread. I read
a thriller instead
of planning my lessons.
Nibble three cookies
in the dusty swirls of light.

Living alone, I am
prone to spectrophobia.
My heart senses the wax
and wane of each moon.
Shadows drift through
my mind like spent coins.

By 2am my heart becomes
a light switch. The footsteps
grow slighter, but never silent.
Each time I turn a page,
my skin seems to shiver.
Each time I blink,
my lashes are spider legs.

ROSES

I set my mouth on fire
when the journey turned cold.
I set my mouth on fire
but you didn't hear me

screaming. God beware the
heavy-hearted woman.
The disappointed, hellishly
dismayed. Lungs charred

by the scorch of too many
bruises. Bruises down the spine
as big as roses. Rage
quickening the pulse, time's

sober skin aflame. Here, Fate
said, I've tied a noose around
your prettiness. You are
sentenced to a life of almost

suicides. But the woman with
one eye said, pain can be
soothed. Her face made me
shudder like a jealous sage.

I met her in the courtyard
where my fear was tamed.
Still your mind with a sip, she
said, with a gulp of rain.

CHORUS

Sometimes I remember
that there's a skull under

my skin. My brain and
mind live there too, along

with a village of lusty
thieves, and cannibals

with the kindest hearts,
and whores who view

life as a powder room
in Egypt. These are

the people who shake
their tins at me, begging

for spare change, as I
sit here biting my tongue

while you chant your
century of self-discoveries

at my nubile ears, which
hardly twitch, even though

a hundred tin cans are
screeching a chorus.

GHAZAL FOR JURY DUTY

I want a ruffled black dress with lace trim.
In dark colors I feel stronger, my face trim.

I've walked twenty-two miles on a sudden whim.
I've touched many wild thoughts, my trace trim.

I like shoes that make me feel like I'm floating.
I used to rush, but I've slowed down, my pace trim.

I steam my polyester suit for jury duty.
Put on glasses and lipgloss, my case trim.

My alter-ego protects me from vampires.
My subconscious is a courtroom, the space trim.

Most arguments are rarely yin or yang.
The truth is a gray vest with lace trim.

ANXIETY

You love brushing your hair in front
of the mirror and remembering
such a simple thing can bring

you joy, even as the fear pushes
against your jugular, even as the
headlines threaten to destroy.

LONE DRIVER

The spinster who hosts my reading
sends me down the wrong lane.

The scenic route, she insists, will make
a shorter ride home. But the road bends

long, leading nowhere. The cell phone
inert in my grip. Mountains, twists, trees.

I pass an abandoned gas station and
shudder. Sometimes driving by myself,

there is a wildness to my thoughts. The
sun heads west with reluctance. Anyone

who might care if I went missing is dozens
of miles away. My knees quiver beneath

the gray skirt. I fear the car's old tires may
rupture. Damn the pushy salespeople of the

world. I'd sensed she found my city ways vulgar.
The sandy sky, inauspicious, hints danger.

TRIVIAL

You should probably
be trying harder, brushing

up on your pop culture
references, learning

to un-introvert. Instead,
you order a cola, not a beer,

like you're supposed to.
And half the night, you

fish for poems in your
mind. They rarely ask

about your life. Their
sideways glances suggest

they find you odd.

CRIME SCENE

I've traveled to morgues and back
but I don't understand the secret
lives of mannequins. These motionless
models like hourglass queens.

Passing by shops, I quash jealousy.
Resist their queer celebrity. No brothel
whores, but still threatening. The
impeccable faces cast a daunting spell.

Sometimes I stop on the sidewalk
to unravel mottled schemes.
Mannequin-me. I stand still, studying.
A detective in a mug shot dream.

Mannequin-three. Lids shaded blue,
but no sleep dust, winks that beam.
Gazing at the world with unblinking
eyes. Their smiles a meld of murder

and make-up. Sometimes they lure
me in. I scrutinize the corpses in the
anxious yellow light. Dresses shimmer
on their hangers like moonlit lakes.

These painted humans, unable
to envy. Their smug mouths sincerely
self-assured. Proud, invulnerable,
they're impossible to kill.   In the fitting

room, I button a white blouse, think
of movies where men curry home dolls.
Embrace, unwittingly, a model mold.
Is this how a girl should be? Mute

ornament, flickering in a void?
No teddy bear tenderness. Un-furry,

un-soft, a vixen selling gleam. *Should*
I buy this shirt? Does it mannequin me?

ICE PICK

I wonder if you've
imagined murdering
me. I see this circus
in your eyes when you
look at me—a royal
disdain for whatever
it is about you I'm
unwilling to affirm.
But my years as Vazir,
Viceroy, and eunuch
are over. This isn't
a Mughal court, though
my thoughts bend
noble. I drift on this
island of love, inside
my cloud of second acts.
It's a place you can't
picture, even with that
ice pick gaze of yours
that seems ready to
stab my neck each
time I say, I'm a wildly
introverted woman.

RECLUSE

A memory to starve like a moth.
The heat melts my resolve. A sip
of water for this cottonmouth.

Echoes blacken between my
thoughts. Nights like this,
my heart pumps fog. Each

incubated recollection, a soldier.
Imagine the force of an image
that marches south, like a fist

pounding at a door. The past
a pen that bleeds ink. Don't
tell me that sleeping alone doesn't

make you anxious. Hollow sounds
crane my throat. I've lived since
childhood in this quaking house.

You have been here too. The door
a paperweight at 3am. The moon
so close, the mind feels stalked.

LOVE STORY

Their knees   brush
on the couch   talking horror films
he compliments   her watch
kisses her   softly
on the cheek   at midnight
says   he should probably leave
when it's time   she leads him
out of   the apartment
into the hallway   where the light
is snow   through the stairwell
she'll show him   the exit
he is so tall   she blushes
he is behind her   as they
descend   the steps
she can sense   his breath
on her shoulders   they drift outside
into the night   where she
unlocks the gate   he says
he's got it   from here
not her style   but she
kisses him   he kisses her back
like he's been   waiting
they kiss & kiss   in the darkness
until she   pulls away
& heads back   her mouth buzzing.

SLASHER

blade breast scream
blood. sane stalker

alone dark. vacant
house shower skin.

stab killer strangle
bone. lust night

moon drunk. red
white nude rain.

creeper mask door
lane. sex saws slashed

veins. nine then just
one. all but one slain.

MUSE NOIR

Every time I write, I sense his hand sliding
up my thigh. Blackening each metaphor, he hammers
my good-girl past until it shatters like a glass mug.

I can't shrug him away. One night in Lahore
when I was fifteen, he climbed beside me in bed,
fastened a palm around my wrist. It was the only

time I saw his face, the square brown chin
and espresso-stained grin, the cunning smile that
colonized my head. I said, *When I get back*

to California, I'll grind you up like a bean. But
he just waved a palm-sized cross and proposed.
I said yes, of course. Still he stood me up

for prom. I wore the ruby dress with the side
slit and waited on the porch. Waited and waited
until my thoughts took off their heels and like a corpse

stood still. For months he did not show. I spent
the evenings sketching black tulips, drinking coffee–
the café the one place he was likely to be–the air

prayer-whipped with the nuns who liked to visit,
play chess in the corner. There the lighting was
lunar. One night, reading a ghost story in the back,

my thoughts woke electric. I put on lipstick,
pressed it on even too. His hand gripped my neck.
The fear delicious, the joy rose up so fast,

I couldn't move. *If I stay*, he said,
you'll carry delusions, make mad like
Edgar Allen Poe. I told him I wasn't the kind

of girl who wanted a rose. He laughed at my quiver,

handed me a silver ring, something gothic. We
didn't kiss. It would have been uncouth

with the nuns watching. But the verdict
was in. My conscience mugged by a thief, I was
wife to spinning dark, to gunfire on the street.

MEAN GIRL

She orders a pound
of shrimp at the deli,

her red hair, a border.
I wonder if each

strand has been
torched into place.

My dark locks unruly,
I draw no lines.

Sometimes we run
into people from our

past who vaguely
remember us.

Her smile dismissive,
the smalltalk feels

forced. I hate that
standing beside her

in my black dress,
waiting to order salmon,

I try to keep the
conversation going.

ENOUGH ABOUT YOU

I drift beside you
in my gray coat, thinking
gray thoughts, down a street
clouded by sunlight.
I listen without blinking.
Plot songs, sing plot twists
while you talk,
my tongue baking
suicides.
       You say,
What if this
whole city leaned
on eggshells? No
nightingales, just pulses.
No ears, just voices.
Each day a wave
of romantic complications?
       I dream the backbone
of a bear, the mouth
of a snake.
But I won't fault myself
for cracking. I
haunt my thoughts
like a ghost. Feel
invaded when you state
your self-absorbed questions.

SHARDS OF WIND

People mock
>> your size
your shape
>> the hair
on your
>> body, the
clothes
>> you choose
to cover
>> your skin.
Their words
>> like shards
of wind
>> have broken
you. But
>> you have
been the
>> aggressor.
too. Active
>> or passive,
you break.

MY BODY IS A LAKE

I am not the woman
I expected to be.

I am not as wise
as I suspected.

I am the hand placing
this tea bag inside

a teacup. The ear
listening while trying

not to get injured.
My body is a lake

where complexities
thrive. What feels

like shame turns
out to be sadness

when I stop doing
the things that I love.

INFJ

I unpack each box
thinking of his lips
on my body

each meditative kiss,
an anchor.

This home, so much
bigger than the one
I left behind.

This lover, so
much closer to
the wind inside of me.

Sometimes sitting
in the same room
for hours we do not speak.

When I cry, he
offers me his arms.
Says, Yes, I know.
These humans are
exhausting.

THE COLLISION

takes place   before 7am
the sky   unconscious
my mind   a thumbprint
I step   into traffic
stunned   as an airplane
after turbulence   my throat
has shrunk   so much
I cannot feel it   no scratches
but fate   hangs in the air
like a glare   a crude statement
the other driver   my head in pieces
you lie   in the grass
a human leaf   suddenly speechless
my heart races   with impatience
I speak words   like insurance
and registration   whispering the questions
as though already   half-dead.

ASYLUM

The shops shine bright with
sweaters, people, lights. It's later

when we drift outside, that my
mind begins to split. My

shoulders tighten, the strip
mall voracious as a Sphinx.

The chatter of strangers
startles me, they seem to hurry

like wild ghosts. Cars fume
through the busy lot, a woman

with streaks of eyeliner walks
by, her red hair scooped into

a nest. Your hand grips mine
in this den of sleepwalkers.

When will we wake up? My
patience could be a leaf about

to wither. I am bewildered
by sudden noises. A driver

honks his horn. I shatter.
Pedestrians drift by and scatter.

YOUNG WOMEN

Neighbor, it's a full moon
and I've seen a man's shadow
drift behind your duplex.

It's just past midnight and
I'm entering the home beside
yours. I pour myself a glass

of juice and slip into bed,
wearing my college sweatshirt.
Alone, I jot introspections in my

notebook, watch television.
Later, on the phone
with a friend, I hear someone

running across the courtyard,
screaming. A moment later,
there's a pounding at my door.

I do not open it. I sit with my
heart in my mouth, remembering
the shadow, how its swaying

beneath the stars in Tucson
was almost lyrical, and how
just nineteen and still learning

my way in a new city, I would
sometimes forget that real
dangers lurk young women.

JANE EYRE IN HOLLYWOOD

Like a blush which rises
to the surface of my skin.
A sinking so final, I swear
I'm drifting to the bottom
of some pit. The barmaid
smiling beneath the lights
          could be Mrs. Ingram about

to spill her drink, the room
so harum-scarum I'm
sure I'll never hold hedonism
the way I hold the quiet calm
of a book, the humans so
bloated tonight I fear
          they might erupt like an

applause. My coat is my
cape in this island of halter
tops. As a child I sketched
angels in my notebook,
hoping one would guide
me through the night,
          still I ended up in this

underworld of strangers
where the curled mouths
glitter like a cloud of coins.
If this is Xanadu, I am as
steady as Rochester's
wife. If this is happiness,
          lock my heart in an attic.

TONGUE-TIED

This time I offer tea to the monsters
in my dreams. Say, "Sugar and milk?"
but they don't answer me. I nod knowingly
at their three-eyed faces, try not to stare
at the worms crawling around their heads.
When the walls turn red, their faces glow
marshmallow green. All night long, they remain
mute and serene. It's a relief, I admit,
not to hear them speak. Their pupils
are cryptic, like the windows of a haunted
shed. There's so much to ask them, but often
I'm tongue-tied by distrust. It's openly
known that monsters don't carry passports.
Their mutterings, when audible, are like
the screechings of unwanted cats. I've
lived enough to know their silence
precedes violence. Still it's easy to get
stumped by the bruises on their necks.

II.
LIGHT

VULNERABLE

I want to
show you
the places
under my skin
where I
was taught
to hold love close.

HANDLE WITH CARE

My porcelain
mouth breathes
porcelain thoughts—
delicate as moon songs,
red as strange loves.

I drift through this
supermarket of strangers.
this wretched beast
inside of me whispering
through my arteries.

My porcelain heart
moves up and down
the staircase of my spine.
Sometimes its beats
take me down porcelain
streets, where it seems
my whole life
might break apart.

Just a slight smile
could shatter
my porcelain teeth
when the sky turns gray.

When clouds gather
in the aisle of my mind,
eyebrows withering into space,
just a blink could burst
my porcelain eyes—
just a shiver might shatter
my porcelain face.

DEMON

A body in pain is a mind in torment. You wake up to a war waging inside of you. The cars outside your home seem to wheel faster and faster. Slower than a slug, you get out of bed, aching for a normal day. If god were a taxi driver, you'd ask for a teacher discount. But still the day's chores must get done. You won't give in to lethargy. You place a dozen carnations in a vase. Fold the laundry in the bedroom. Thinking about the person you once were, you shudder at the clownish desperation. When you watch horror films, you shudder at the sight of blood. A psychic once told you, *stay calm, my dear. You're surrounded orbs of light.* Sometimes, you can feel a demon pressing against your skull, but there's also this white music.

THE IRONY IS

The simpler
the clothes,
the louder
the mind.

The darker
the thought,
the whiter
the words.

The slower
the kiss,
the faster
the falling.

The deeper
the feeling,
the stranger
the need.

The weaker
the coffee,
the stronger
the cup.

The fiercer
the wind,
the softer
the sky.

The grayer
the mood,
the brighter
the dress.

The colder
the shoulder,

the hotter
the chest.

STRANGERS

As January turns
a corner, the world eases

into a new year,
donning ironed shirts

and trousers. I imagine
you getting drunk and

wonder if you ever think of me.
I hope that you don't.

We are essentially
strangers, and I cannot

forgive what you did,
though one day I'll

plant tulips. Pink,
white, and yellow ones.

DREAMCATCHER

Most of the time
I digress in my thinking.
The leaves look vague
outside my bedroom window.
I don't tell anyone
that I own a tree shaped heart.
So many of us
are suspicious of trees
and people—
the way they take root
in the spine and call
attention to themselves,
but this car I just bought
is the electric blue
of a Spanish mosque.
There are cities in my blood
no map can claim.
I grip the steering wheel
as though letting go might
mean falling. My eyes
are brown but receptive
to every color they see.
I want to eat a history
book, I tell the palm trees.
Have I mentioned
the moon yet? It tends
to surface whenever
I enter language, as though
driving down the 405
in Los Angeles could
be a pilgrimage of sorts,
my cobalt car, a dreamcatcher.

CLICK

When people like my posts,
I feel the dopamine rush.

Here's a picture of me
reading Charlotte Bronte,

wearing a Jason mask.
I wonder what others

make of it when the
image pops up in their feed.

And the ones who don't
click, are they offended?

Am I unfriended? Sometimes
my shadow will text:

I've been waiting all day.
Why haven't you liked my post?

MAGNIFYING GLASS

There is the agony of carrying
an untamed mind, watching
the stars shrink and shriek
in the ubiquitous sky of the mind,

feeling the sun crack open
at the wrists where moons collide.
Reflection is that dull clicking
at the end of a tunnel. Crisper

than snow, it eats itself
like a wolf—explodes into a bomb
beneath a magnifying glass.
God, some believe, formed the world,

but what rides the gallop of the mind?
Each stride, an unresolved
argument that reaches for elegant
peaks, in streaks of suicides.

SEMI-TROPICAL

As summer peaks into August, the palm
trees become inspired ghosts, swaying
in the heat. By now I've learned one can't
make a season move faster. It will claim

its space on the calendar, which in most
cases means someone feels neglected.
At sunrise, I drift hazily out of bed
as though this palm tree inside of me

knows its ancestors lived elsewhere.
I step into the island of my living room.
The weather in my mind, semi-tropical.
What would Los Angeles be without its

gilt and glamour, the ancient freeways
and aquamarine breeze? Sipping coffee
on my 2nd floor patio, I gaze up at the
lively fronds across the street. My heart

could drink a small ocean. How would
my mornings be without the simple allure
of these trees? A car wheels down the lane
below, leaving dusky traces of its journey.

EXISTENTIAL CRISIS

For a month I tiptoe
around this city
and fill my journal
with question marks.

SUMMER FORGETS TO WEAR A PETTICOAT

I bought the straw hat with black ribbon, thinking
about Sherlock Holmes. Sometimes I wear

it on walks around the neighborhood.
The buildings & vacant schools don't resemble

Baker Street. In my twenties, I drank a lot of tea:
PG Tips—a dash of milk, a spoonful of sugar.

Why do habits form then suddenly vanish? Sometimes
friendships—whole cities disappear. Last week

a flash of lightning struck Venice Beach. Even summer
forgets to wear a petticoat when clouds appear.

It's easier to swim and surf without a shield. I never
took a statistics course, but on evening walks

I probe the data of my life. In the absence of green,
clues & hints remain unseen, flare on impulse.

VILLAIN

Who is the crazy one:
you or the woman
you consider to be
your villain, her
bright eyes haunting?

Sometimes when you
press around
your heart, you fear
the love has
tripled.

You tell yourself,
the heart has
no room for monsters.
But the aorta
only listens

to the waning
of the moon.

REHAB CENTER FOR GOD ADDICTION

The sufferers came day after day lugging
their drug free suitcases, fanning themselves

with new science books. No Gods Exist,
the sign read. And there came random searches

for bibles and prayer mats, crosses and sacred beads.
Any sign of worship, and they kicked you out.

Reading scripture's a waste, they said. An addiction
like meth. Snort these lines quick, and you'll end up

a murderer. Each patient was branded "atheist",
and therapists led group talks where people cried

over years of blind dependence, obsession
with priests. Everything's random, the doctor

said. Our bodies made from stardust. Isn't this
miracle enough? Abortion clinics get defamed

by the addicted. Fundamentalism circles the globe.
But the days stretched long at rehab, and people

struggled with the dizzying sense of freedom.
Mealtimes triggered some to press palms together,

and for this they locked you in a room to watch
documentaries about the Taliban, the Crusades.

Our bodies are water and dust, the doctor said. God
worship's a disease. There's no proof of a creator's hand.

Everyone must agree. Still it was acceptable to sit
by the koi pond at dusk and stare up at the moon, even

read your horoscope. Fine to write a song that praised
the mystery of the galaxy & sprang from nothingness.

SELF-DOUBT

There are times
you wonder
if you're going crazy.
Like a noose, your mind
knots around itself
until it chokes.
But even the sky
quakes when the moon
seems hidden, fears
its eye's eloped.

FLIRT

floozy chick tease.
cougar eye-candy

yogamom queen.
whore hussy handmaiden

homegirl. psychobitch sass
single-mom swinger.

spouse spinster nag
stripper. mistress mother

sweetheart bitch. bird
butch bridezilla & babe.

Sexism persists.
who is to blame?

SATURDAY MORNING

I stumble into the kitchen craving
coffee while you sleep. The room seems
to be floating. I wonder if I am dreaming.
But when I pinch myself, nothing happens. I
shiver a little in the air conditioned room.
It's too early for the sun outside the window
to warm me. My cell vibrates, but the number's
unfamiliar. Who is calling? A neighbor?
A distant friend? I am curious but don't answer.
The coffee tastes good, but I am out of creamer.
I prefer my coffee milky. It seems pessimistic,
to drink one's coffee without some sweetness.
Bugger. I will have to walk to the store,
make small talk with the cashier about yesterday's
fires. The thought makes me want to get
back into bed. But I grab my jacket off the
dining chair, then brush my teeth. My purse
is on the counter. I reach inside it for my
debit card, which is always somewhere
near the bottom. Saturday morning I spend
the first few hours of my day reading, then listen
for ghosts. They have been visiting more
recently, whispering on occasion. At first
this frightened me, but I am no longer
bothered by their imperceptible footsteps.
You are sleeping in the room next door.

GROWTH

It's as if you're not sure
who that was, the person

you were five years ago,
the injustices you permitted.

It's as if that person who
couldn't stop moving and

making plans was fleeing a
downpour. You don't recognize

her—that silly girl, though
a part of you knows you had

to be her and fall again
and again to get here.

QUESTION

What if I'm the subject
of an experiment, and half
this city is watching me,
and the intuitions I've had
about holding some people
at a distance are not unresolved
psychological traumas but
just good basic instincts?

TWO VOICES

Sometimes you wake up
to sadness in your mind.
Nothing has happened yet,
and you are already hopeless.

The things you think about
to feel angry come singing
to the surface, and now the
coffee doesn't taste so

good anymore, and you
can suddenly sense your
impatience with the world,
the buzzing phones and

mounting traffic. You find
your optomism stuttering.
Sometimes you let yourself
pray then judge yourself

for engaging in some
antiquated practice. Other
times you decide to let yourself
be angry. Because wouldn't it

be toxic to push these feelings
down now? Though mostly
what upsets you is something
you could never control. This is

when you start to notice that
there are two voices inside
of you. The cynic who gets angry,
and the poet who observes.

BAKER IN WINTER

By then I'd suspected
my shadow could bake,
which made me feel invisible.

In December, the kitchen
counters showcased
flour, sugar, and vanilla.

Melting the chocolate
in a little pot, I thought
of the Grand Canyon.

Whipping the cream
with a beater, I thought
of the North Pole.

Cold gathered inside
our house. The Christmas
tree became a fireplace.

In the oven, batter
baked into chocolate
cake. And in that alchemy,

the shadow disappeared.
You noticed the cocoa
stains on my apron.

EVERYTHING NEW

That night, I couldn't escape menace.
I stared down at the dripping faucet
in my kitchen, cursing under my breath.
The evening had been a fickle light bulb.
A long conversation with my mother sparked
by the flames of our tongues, the phone
heavy in my hands as the light seesawed
on and off. The whole house shook like
the belly of a lamp nudged by a careless hip.

I had worn a night like this before where
darkness thickened behind the shades, where
I was the skin and the veil, the nut
and the wrench. I spotted a spider teasing
out a web in my dining room, and later
sifting through *saris* in the closet, my fingers
pressed over dust, and I imagined each garment
in the tomb of its own unwearing,
like the weeks when no light bulbs glowed
inside me, and there were piles of memories
on my desk. I had managed with my khakis
and cotton tees, the odd dress which suggested
I had the fleeting charm of a tourist.

But that night, in Los Angeles, I made sure
to touch the green-lipped hems, even the turquoise
shawl my mother handed me once as a wish.
Scarf by scarf, shoe by shoe, I spelled a prayer
with my hands, making everything new,
even the belts and the caps. Even that too small
ruffled skirt I once bought from a clothing store in Lahore
with all the white of a summer cloud
between my eyes, light fusing with my breath.

FOCUS

Judgment is a camera.
A fancy camera
with a good lens.
Aim and shoot,
the cynic says.
And look how black
the trees seem
suddenly, as though
pretending to be green
for the tourists.
We are all tourists here,
a friend once told me,
lifting a tuna roll
between her chopsticks.
I wondered if I'd misjudged
her my whole life
because sitting there
in the mellowed light
of the restaurant, she
sounded so meta.

WHISPERS

Bella's left eye was plugged shut, pressed permanently asleep. A birth defect, her father explained one night dipping *naan* in curry sauce.

They were our neighbors in Building One. In the corridor, Bella played hopscotch with my sister and me, placed stones I'd picked out of the Red Sea near Jeddah. Her right lid fluttered when she laughed. I pretended not to be afraid.

Whiter than rain, her Norwegian skin glistened. She'd grip her father's hand, glance up at him, pride in eye. Whisper *Bismillah* as if ordering a scone, her family a puzzle of Muslim converts.

Peering out our third floor window in Taif, I'd gaze down at dead cats in the alley. Count corpses with taps on glass. What had happened to Bella's mother? Some weeks there were kittens. I didn't want to look but stared every afternoon, hoping to see a clear space in the shade.

Two days after my ninth birthday, Bella spent the night. Aboo was in Riyadh. In our kitchen, near the framed picture of the Ka'ba, Ami fried peas, sauced chicken. My sister set the table. Over dinner, slicing chicken with a knife, Bella confessed she was a sleepwalker.

Later I couldn't sleep. I crept into my mother's bed. Lay awake, listened for shadows. Pictured Bella's hand reaching for a knife, her lips mouthing *Bismillah* as she roamed the hallway. An alley of darkness behind her left lid.

CONFETTI

The cynic, the romantic, the fool,
and the feminist. I have been them all,

and I have been them well. But
I am happier when I am not

thinking which words best describe
me, for I am more than adjectives. I am

story. I am this tender-hearted drive
to turn the world inside out, this

delicate force that sometimes hugs
itself so tightly, the fears seem to break

apart, and all my thoughts are moons
orbiting a planet of plot twists that

unfurl and intersect. Look how many
subplots there are and notice how

the exposition keeps changing fonts
as though hoping to scatter like confetti.

DETECTIVES IN THE SAMOSA SHOP

I ordered mint & tamarind—my nose in a book. Who had poisoned this country girl: the maid, an errant lover? Each paragraph kept me guessing.

A cryptic buzz in the restaurant, but I didn't notice the detectives until page sixty-four. The waitress placed a basket on my table, two servings of chutney.

But suddenly I wasn't hungry. Like a costume party, the faces perplexed. Columbo? Jane Marple? Was that Sherlock Holmes seated across Poirot?

I watched them dip & crunch, savor the cumin scent. Each seemed pensive, lost in some conundrum. Even the painted women in saris, red bangles at their wrists, appeared to puzzle over the room's conspicuous silence.

Soon Wallander drifted in as though Los Angeles were some Swedish pit stop. Then Nancy Drew in her plaid dress & headband, a girlish hurry in her step. I tried reading the next chapter, but now the restaurant presented a greater mystery.

One server turned up the Bollywood music. The door swung again: Sam Spade. Philip Marlowe. Even Father Brown, on the quest for Indian pastry. Each ordered the lunch special: two samosas, a cup of chai.

When Jessica Fletcher came by, I was ready to confess I wanted her autograph. I stopped myself from shouting "murder" to make her turn her head.

But this sudden convention of sleuths seemed oblivious that the dining room had become a synchronistic meeting place. It was April. The sun poured in through the windows, eager to illuminate mislaid clues.

THE WEATHERMAN'S TEXT

My solution to seasickness:
become a champagne pink cloud.

Once at a dinner party in Austin
I sat beside a woman whose

mouth became the sea. I hadn't
discovered cloud-me yet,

so I went home with a fire in my head.
For too many years, I walked

without leg warmers, treated
the Milky Way as a scientific fact.

But now at dinner parties,
I speak Galaxy during small talk.

Observations about the weather
seem too narcissistic. Freud

believed sex was always the
subtext. Too much talk about

the universe would have made
him guess, *penis envy*. Once

I almost died on the North Sea.
The ferry rocked through

the night as if writing a suicide
note. I couldn't fall asleep until

the weatherman texted me,
become a champagne pink cloud.

DAMSEL GHOST

Every city girl could use a boat.
And a lake. And an empty afternoon
to sail out west. Which is why

I put on the white dress, the one
I'd bought at an estate sale, grabbed
my childhood quilt, and brushed

my hair till it shook. I hung a lantern
on the prow and let the winds
lead the way. Nobody knew I was

fleeing. I'd tossed my cell away
in the laundry pile, my flip-flops
in the sink. No I wasn't drunk.

I didn't drink. But I'd been looking
at these pictures of swans all morning,
wishing I'd been born with a longer

neck. Someone who could freely
drift up the coast. Someone who
didn't live on cigarettes and toast.

But here I was, escaping the magic
monotony of my life. No one's wife,
no one's mother. Just a damsel ghost.

The trees hung gray. The sun
a shadowed eye blinking. The good
news was the boat drifted long,

didn't sink. And I felt tall and wild—
three candles lit. My breathing
slowed. I was miles from L.A. The day

was water, mountains, air, and I'd
escaped. No insight came, but this I knew:
Every city girl could use a boat. A white

dress and a lake. And an afternoon quilted
with golden thread, after a morning
in bed staring at photographs of swans.

LOTUS

Like a fleeting headline I've vanished, declined
        invitations. Scissored

on the sofa, I write slogans till midnight, chant
        mantras with my hand.

Bedtime, I glance at my former self, posing
        plugged in a picture I have found

scrolling through Facebook on my cell. Some
        nights I tint my hair with schemes,

dust the boots I once worn to a loud 70's bar
        in Hollywood. Some nights I paint

my nails the blood orange of a mango, light rooms
        with my petticoat laughter. Slowly,

I'll appear again, palms pinking warmth, skin taut
        as a blade. Accidental

meetings at the grocery, they question me.
        Fingering the tomatoes,

they slice me thin with their eyes. How the
        easy dereliction? What

the something making me red? Only this used thread,
        I say pointing

at my past, a mind I've tucked like a bribe between
        the knees of my chest.

Now I have this lotus, this altar inching wide. Now
        the world, for better

or worse, has swallowed the gossiping circles.
        Sometimes I wake

early to watch the sun rising from the second
        floor patio. The sun is

a sloth. Its shifts are subtle like the breath.
        Inhaling, exhaling

I feel myself drawing light, the furtive turn
        of my neck.

MY GOTHIC ROMANCE

The sun grows wider every
day until we breathe
in an oven. You rifle
through the medicine

cabinet, but the
little pills take you
elsewhere. I throw out
half my clothes, start

over. Then the accident,
the surgery, and those
nights we sleep with
one eye open. I feel

your heartbeat when
you pull me close. Think
of the day we first
met. On Thanksgiving,

we bake a whole chicken.
I fold the laundry while
you paint the door frame.
Our home is an altar

where small rituals
light candles. In winter,
your body is the cape
that keeps me warm.

POET'S BLOOD

I am timid book-slut on the quest
for an out of the box red.
Something gothic or slack.
At the makeup counter,
the saleswoman reeks
of a beauty pageant.
Every tube I touch belongs
in a queen's boudoir.
In my beige bedroom I drink
coffee, read pages—long or short.
Lipstick leaves a pretty scar
when I kiss passages I love.
Glossy, matte, or sheer?
Maybe something Van Gogh
would smear across a canvas.
A force with grandiloquence,
like an immigrant: *Japanese*
Lilly, Icelandic Apple,
Maltese Rouge. The mirror
at the counter seems to approve
them all. *Persian Rose,*
Arabian Night. The one
I pick could be a black
bookmark with golden trim.
Even at this age, I am a high
school jejune who slugs Emily
Dickinson. But the salesperson
wins: *Poet's Blood*, she says,
leaves metaphors on the lips.
Each literary sip, a couplet.

REMNANTS

Astronomy depends on random conversations
in supermarkets. Ask any stargazer:

there is a need for plain communication.
Every syllable uttered in the routine vernacular

carries wind chimes of galaxy.
Still, the memories leap as I step

in line at checkout twelve. Across from me
the magazines speak in glossy whispers.

Stars airbrushed and suntanned.
Once the pages ignited childhood dreams.

But now I don't ask the bright
images to bring me constellations.

When the cashier says, credit or debit,
his words are a consolation. So much

we drift in staggers beyond our senses.
The night sky a silhouette of empty parks.

It's a blessing to be asked a manageable question,
to speak the answer without a planet

weighing down the tongue. The stars
watching from above catch remnants

of their sparks in our daily exchanges.
As scientists, focusing their telescopes,

stand on the shoulders of functional speech
to forge pathways to the unexplained.

LIZARDS

By the time you realize you love the color
green, at an age by which you should've

already known, at an age by which everyone
has reproduced, or bought a house, or filed for

bankruptcy, you finally understand your mission:
being a sponge for stories—and happily the world

is overflowing with them—because your alter
ego is a detective. And what you've come

to see is that enlightenment is observation,
so what's happening around you could be as

shocking as a naked man inside a library, waving
a leash, because the content's less significant

than the person actually looking. Because as
a relative of the color blue, green conjures oceans,

trees, and the envious hearts of lizards, you
suspect that everything you encounter is a clue.

HOLD MY HAND, MARGARET ATWOOD

After "In the Secular Night"

If I needed a hitman,
I'd hire you, drag you
to a pool hall where we'd
drink beer and talk business,
speak swear words as punctuation.
You'd tell me the truth,
how writing novels
wasn't the crux. You
wanted to work for easy
cash under the table,
wander the earth dressed
like a biker chick.
The night, you say, is secular.
But the morning's
a parking lot of stars—
row after row of constellations.
The white lines twinkle.

AWAKENING

To the guilt in your heart
say, I'm a good person.
To the fear in your heart
say, I'll make an effort
to be my best self.
To the sadness in your
heart say, I'll give myself
the compassion others
never gave me. To the
perfectionism in your
heart say, name one
person who's perfect.

REBIRTH

Last night
I dreamt
my sadness
turned
into light.

Acknowledgments:

The following poems, sometimes in earlier drafts, have appeared or will appear in the following publications:

-"Ice Pick" in *Strange Horizons* (Fall 2018)

-"Recluse" in *The Paddock Review* (Summer 2018)

-"Semi-Tropical" (forthcoming) in *Liminality: A Magazine of Speculative Poetry* (Spring 2018)

-"Red Moon" in *Moira* (2017)

-"Enough About You" in *Moira* (2017)

-"Serpentine" in *The Literary Hatchet* (2017)

-"Thornfield" in *The Literary Hatchet* (2017)

-"The Weatherman's Text" in *Pedestal Magazine* (2016)

-"Damsel Ghost" (and "Muse Noir") in the *Pacific Coast Poetry Series'* anthology of Los Angeles Poets (2015)

-"Remnants" in *Pedestal Magazine* (2014)

-"Muse Noir" appeared in *The 5-2 Crime Poetry Weekly* (2014)

-*"Everything New"* in *Mascara Literary Review* (2011)

-"Hopeless Romantic" in *Strange Cargo* (2010)

The following poems, sometimes in earlier drafts, appeared in my chapbook, *Summer Forgets to Wear a Petticoat*, published by Finishing Line Press (2016): *Muse Noir, Summer Forgets to Wear a Petticoat, Rehab Center for God Addiction, Detectives in the Samosa Shop*, and *The Weatherman's Text*

The following poems, sometimes in earlier drafts, appeared in my chapbook, *Tongue-tied: A Memoir in Poems*, published by Finishing Line Press (2012): *Whispers, Tongue-tied,* and *Lotus*

A few short poems (or excerpts) from this manuscript have been posted on my Instagram page under the handle *#mygothicromance.* In particular, the following poems: *Anxiety, Shards of Wind, My Body a Lake, INFJ, Vulnerable, Villain, Self-Doubt, Flirt, Growth, Question, Confetti, Awakening,* and *Rebirth*

NOTE: Poems published between 2010 and 2011 were published under a previous last name, "Turner"

With profound gratitude to my parents, Farhana and Afzal, my sister, Naureen, my friend, Erika Ayon, the Los Angeles poetry community, and my colleagues at New Roads School.

A special thanks to Martyn, who has supported my journey, heart and soul, through the crafting of this manuscript. You are my gothic romance.

Mehnaz Sahibzada was born in Pakistan and raised in Los Angeles. She holds an M.A. in Religious Studies from UC Santa Barbara, and she is a 2009 PEN USA Emerging Voices Fellow in Poetry. Her short story, "The Alphabet Workbook", appeared in the August 2010 issue of Ellery Queen Mystery Magazine. Her poetry chapbooks, *Tongue-Tied* (2012) and *Summer Forgets to Wear a Petticoat* (2016), were published by Finishing Line Press. *My Gothic Romance* is her first full-length publication. Her work has appeared in numerous publications, such as *Liminality, Moira, The Paddock Review, The Literary Hatchet,* and *Pedestal Magazine.* A high school English teacher, she lives in southern California.

To learn more visit: www.poetmehnaz.com

www.ingramcontent.com/pod-product-compliance
Lightning Source LLC
Chambersburg PA
CBHW021155090426
42740CB00008B/1098